Crocodile Cliko Cliko

Crocodile Cliko Cliko

Leon McConnell

Resist Entertainment
2022

First Printing: 2022
ISBN 979-8-9853126-0-7
Resist Entertainment
Boyle Heights, California

Cover Art by Prince Johnson

Part 1:

Logic is the size of a human hand

Sometimes we can't see all the good things we have
Because our eyes are looking towards
All of the good things that we want

God is a secret thing inside you
Hopefully hinted at in everything you do

I often wish when we talked
That it was with my left arm stretched out
And your ear close to my heart

The entire earth is an hourglass
Good luck trying to get any footing

I think most artists set out to shine, to let the light in
But I'm just pointing a magnifying glass at the sun

When your trauma makes a home in the dust
Life forces you to clean

To be a tree when you know the fire is coming is to be human

Now and again, your soul reaches out for the one you love
And comes back empty handed

I'd eat you in a second but I hope you get stuck in my teeth forever

Maybe the end of the tunnel is just deeper underground

The path I always wanted to take
Now I see would only have ever taken me so far

You're locked out
I'm burned down

Crocodile Cliko Cliko

A trailblazer doesn't mind burning a bridge or two
A phoenix is fine with setting its whole life on fire
Taking a nap and starting all over again

All I ever wanted was to be turned all the way up and set on fire
Then pushed out of an airplane and let adrift until only ashes
Hit the ground across miles and miles for weeks dissipating
Into the breath of children, exhaled in giggles

You fear death because you can't see beyond yourself
You don't feel god because you refuse to believe
In the concept of a spiritual existence
You're afraid because every second ticks you closer to the end
And you only see your potential for beauty squandered

On the sea of life not everyone gets a lighthouse
Sometimes we surf through bioluminescence
And it's enough that you know what you're swimming in is beautiful
But not light enough to see what lies ahead
So, we move by touch and grow accustomed to the dark

When the world stops spinning
A definite lack of surprise is unearthed
Human curiosity probes darkness
To feel the things we could never see

I've retreated
Gone three levels back
Deep deep deep into the quiet
Slowly severing my support system
Calmly sawing my plank away from the stage
I'm ready to drift away

I've been a run on sentence since my mom missed her first period, screaming every thought but you ain't hearing it. Life inside my head ain't the dreariest thing that I could muster but I must've lost some luster along the way somewhere now that I'm a suspect in crimes of passion set adrift into the ether in the most apathetic fashion. In other words, shit's boring.

To ignore the spirit because it can't be held by a machine, man's way
Of trying to control his surroundings, doesn't disprove the spirit
It only further evidences how frightened men are of losing control

I pay attention like karma to the deepest debts owed to actions over
the course of a lifetime accrued in tiny increments and read like you
were written in the thoughts of moths onto moonbeams across a
forest. With the flip of a switch butterflies become jet engines. Hold
my hand while we rip through the skies.

The concept that great pressure is to be valued because it's what turns
coal into diamonds reflects only the notion that humans think every-
thing exists to serve their purposes and that the highest purpose is
being able to acquire something useless and shiny.

The motivation that moves each individual in the human equation
may not be the sum painted on their face. Someone may be showing
the world twos while they're driven by imaginary numbers, pushing
the world where they want it, unseen. This is why all problems are
factored for the unknown.

Me, I live in this moment
In a line of moments I rebirth
As if all existence
Were just breath on a string
Wrapping around a flat earth

You think your answers are the right answers
But you don't even know what questions are being asked
Or who's asking them
Or what language they're speaking
You're seven dimensions from the truth
Insisting you're breathing an absolute

Perhaps the different religions of the world are trying to explain who
the one God is the same way the different languages of the world are
trying to explain what the one sun is, or the one sky.

Crocodile Cliko Cliko

The smell of pussy on my fingers and on my face, in my bed can't be washed away. The sounds of elation, of joy affected, your screams, these energies have become poltergeists, alive unto themselves. These dreams fucking in a corner, they haunt me.

Nights we run through
Are the exclamation points on this life sentence
But I don't think I can run through the night with you
This is where our stories part

You think confidence is shiny?

The way petroleum companies
Have oil spills and destroy oceans
Entertainment companies make movies
And destroy people

I never understood why anyone
Would want to be an astronaut
When all the aliens are here on planet earth
And everyone is so completely unexplored

Trying to make anything work with some people
Is like trying to form words from two different alphabets

People want something to buy into
And that is generally not themselves

Don't be someone who stands on beaches and talks about oceans

Even the prayers of ants reach the ears of god

All of religion, theology, and philosophy is just a child
Explaining rocket science to a toddler

You crave stability but life is dynamic, like the sea
There will always be waves, lulls, and storms

Be kind. Just be kind. Be kind to other people. Be kind to animals. Be kind to yourself. Take a split second before you react. The best thing that could happen in this world would be if everyone was kind. It'd transform everything.

The struggle is between those who value life
And those who only value themselves
That's what it always will be

Some days I can barely raise my head up from the ashes

Every time you drop a baby on its head a police officer is born

You can try to get out of the hole into a better world
Or you can make the world in the hole better

Fantasy is played out under spotlights
The world is changed in the dark

When you realize that the Israelites wandered through the desert for forty years because it took them that long to learn a lesson
you start to see the desert all around you

A warm body
A cold bottle
A busy house
A well run machine
Are all the same thing
Just a human being testing their limits
Just a person making sure they're still alive

What's murmured in their hearts is never spoken from their lips
...let me hurt you so I can love you

You want an adventure
You want to ride a wild wave of life until it crashes
Laugh and walk away a little sore smiling
I know you
You want to be in love, madly in love and lose control
You want life to tumble into the setting horizon
And stumble unseen happy into the forest

Crocodile Cliko Cliko

Part 2:

1.

Love is an obsession, a seed, a poisonous flower eating at all that makes you human. Love is a morning glory, covering your house, digging into the walls, choking out all reason & children, sacrificing everything to bloom beautiful flowers, blood red sticky, reaching for your eyes, your scent, your fingers, your smile, tearing across fields and fences. Try to remove it. Love will burn through years. Love will drive roots deeper than mitochondria. Love will hide dna in memories, in ghosts you never knew were out there waiting. Love will ride like a disease, like happiness on the backs of rats. Love will infect the timbre of voices, the glimmer of light, the texture of touch, a prick in your nose. Love is a fever inducing hallucinations, covering over the worst of us in pretty dresses, hiding rotten teeth behind the softest lips. Love is a virus, a spell. Love is a witch driving infants from a cliff, cracking open bones and sucking marrow from their soul. Love is the morning star staring into a mirror blinded by its own radiance. Unable to unfurl a blockade against the whirlwind, reason will drown in the storm of love. Countrysides will suffer devastation. Love will malign aeons of logic and basic math when it takes hold of you. Love will drive you full bore towards death ...because God is love and he is waiting for you with open arms.

2.

Lust is gravity
Just outside the big bang
Where all of existence is waiting
And the nothing can't help but thirst

Lust is a hammer dropped from an asteroid
Swallowed by a glass star
Burst into a cosmic spray
So that the lifetime of gods is surpassed
As it echoes off into the new no longer nothings

Lust is a little girl in a back seat
Not giving one fuck that she's at a family reunion

Crocodile Cliko Cliko

It's the need to swallow to expand
To connect over and over
To add an equal sign to your equation
To do the math
To run numbers across finger prints
Licked digits
Drip decimals
Zero after zero
After zero

Lust is the lion god ripping flesh from its savannah mates
Starving to feed
Blood on its tongue
Lust is pure will
Attraction like magic
Conjuring what you need or you'll die

Lust is the earth shaking
Like hips possessed
Spitting magma
Flooding oceans
Burning so hard that new land
Is left in its aftermath

Lust is the demon drums
Chanting feverishly
Sweating your insides
Singeing oxygen
So that the very ether crackles

Lust is a demigod
Pulling on the fabric of mother earth
Rupturing this world's amniotic membranes
Pushing out something new
A reality flipped inside out
Lust is the birther

Lust is the engine
Lust is lips and teeth driven at 100 miles an hour

It's the gasoline fire bath you crawled out of
And drip dried across terra firma

Lust is the scars on your back
The panties in your purse
The very centrifugal force
That all these dinner plates spin and spin and spin

Lust is a snail finding its way across the ocean floor
And lust is the ocean itself skipping across Sumatra
Because someone in a kitchen cooking padang
Looked like they wanted a kiss

    3.

I want to scan your body between my lips
And learn your math
I want to catch the numbers dripping off your breath
Before they evaporate into the great equation
I want to know the pins in your hip
The way I know my own childhood
I want to study you, examine each freckle, each tiny golden hair
While you tell me the you only you know
I want to see the picture of your face glowing by volcano light
That only god saw
I want to be there in the shower
Sorting through your thoughts on the universe
I want to know you like the molecule in your heart
That sits next to the bird of your spirit
On the branch of your soul
I want my ghost to haunt your ghost
I want the way you move across any given room burned into me
I want to learn to savor your pattern of speech
And marvel at the things you don't say
I want to hold onto the tip of your iceberg
And slide down into your sea
I want to freeze against you and be the same cold

4.

Drunk on the streets of Mexico City
Making out on a beach in Hoi An
Adrift under a waterfall in Luang Prabang
Lit in the chaos of Khao San Road
Head out the window, sailing through Null Arbor
Climbing past eagles in Acadia
Meeting a stranger in a parking lot
Somewhere in New Jersey and falling in love
My beach, an hour from the spirit tree
The little waves of Lake Nicaragua as I float from Ometepe
The ruins of Bagan all by myself
A change of planes at the airport in Kuala Lumpur
To take a trip with someone I just met
Four days on a boat to Komodo
A life I had one time in Mazatlan
Rebirth across the Sydney Harbor Bridge
The pixie center of the universe in a storm
With my mom outside of Reykjavik
Childhood in a lagoon
Selling honeysuckle along the side of the road
Eating blackberries off the bush
Reading Kerouac in a grocery store
And deciding I had to see the world
Our scooter and the lighthouse in Formentera
Just like the movie
Being dead sick in London
Being dead sick in Udaipur
Coughing up blood before I got to Darjeeling
Wandering through the Himalayas
And doing cartwheels with little kids
Then playing soccer in a field like it was a dream
Buying heroin in King's Cross and getting ripped off
Going down on a girl at the park in Vancouver
Because I had nothing else to do
Getting my first tattoo with my bestest friends
In Amsterdam on Halloween
Watching a million bats tornado into a chimney in Portland
From the sidewalk

Dancing in ladyboy bars in the Philippines
Like it was what god made me to do
And that was I how worshipped
Adoring splendid souls at the Salton Sea
Happily jumping from rock to rock with you
Standing in front of a tree with a million birds
Somewhere in Belize while I ate ice cream and the sun set
Conversations I barely made my way through in Cartagena
In a language not my own that pulsed with perfect humanity
Oh the humanity!
What gorgeous gorgeous creatures of every shape and color
Awing an entire spectrum
Everywhere I've been they've marched in the street together
United against themselves
I've seen joy in Copenhagen
And made friends in Norway with people I never saw again
I played Monopoly in Transylvania
And danced to Mmmm Bop
With some chubby guy's girlfriend
Because he wanted me to sleep with her
She ran a copy center
His cousin worked at the zoo and got us in for free
We sat and watched the turtles
I skydived with children
And more than once let the sea carry me home
I locked myself away in the Andaman Islands
And waited for trouble to blow over
Knowing all this
Having been constructed in a whirlwind
Sometimes I find it difficult to pin a life down to letters
But I tell you, so that you'll tell me
And when we can't run
We'll have something to read

5.
Times I Fell in Love
On a dancefloor with someone who begged me not to leave
Over the phone with a friend after my cousin had died
In a dark room with a girl who cried before I curled up inside her

---

Crocodile Cliko Cliko

On an island, driving a scooter through the fog
From lighthouse to lighthouse
In a yard on a blanket during a Tuesday afternoon while you giggled
Slowly, while being convinced, perhaps hesitantly
Once while you slept
Once with a soldier through ruins to survive
Often with god when I remember how much I forget again and again
In a mirror across time between bodies
That share a soul but never touch
Sometimes at dogs and children and passers by
Every day with moments
Occasionally in the bath with a passing thought
They never love me long enough to stay
But this is what my heart had to give

6.

Only in love can you be sick and drunk
Overjoyed, morose and overwhelmed
See the world for what it truly is
But be completely blindsided all at once
Only in love can you be on fire, ecstatic with burns
In love I want to speak in tongues and pray to the god inside you
In love I want to push your body like a jet engine
In a child's pocket with reckless caresses to the outer limits
And cover you in sweat and bones
In tiny kisses, my teeth in your shoulders, your hair in my fist
Your soul burning into my soul
Like I was born to stare at the sun until the day I died
I'd be so happy if you killed me
With stories about plants and little giggles,
Three word sentences, spoken concisely
I'd take those wounds
I'd bleed out smiling
I'd worship you till my jaw was broken
I'd study your holy scriptures
I'd write new heresies holding your hand
And carry graven images carved by memory
Across this soul into the afterlife
I'd suck a river Styx from out between your legs

And speak Charon into existence
If that's what it took to sail you from side to side
I want to eat apples in your garden
And watch you grow a paradise
You could turn hades into a warm wet shade simply by showing up
I want to hold pinkies and dangle legs with you
On the banks of Babylonian rivers in captivity
I want to turn whatever bedroom we're in into a heaven
I want to step outside of time holding your hand
And know you the way nature knows god
Amen

7.

My father, who was ungiving, taught me to want nothing
My brother, who was greedy
Taught me not to give everyone everything you can
Because some people will take everything from you
My love, who broke my heart taught me
That sometimes things work better once they've been broken
My life, which is a constant lesson
Taught me that even the deepest wounds
Can form you in the most beautiful and necessary ways
So love even when it will certainly cause you pain
Love those who seem like a lost cause
Love the horrible
Love the dumbest person you know
Love assholes
Love everyone you can
Love them like water loves oceans and bedrock and human bodies
Love them because love is the ether
And matter and breath between all everything
Love like love is the only thing that keeps you alive
Love like history was written in only four letters
Love like there was no end ever and love is the reason

8.

I wanted to devour you
I wanted to drain you
I wanted to worship you with my mouth and fingers

Crocodile Cliko Cliko

And every part of me
I wanted to grab hold of you and rip a hole in space/time
I wanted a drift with you, heartbeat to heartbeat

I want to meet your waves with waves
Put an ocean to the face of your ocean and cross bodies
I want to earn your lust, compound your love
And create something from a bang
That only happens in the mind of god
I want the electricity between those synapses staticked
Through little golden hairs on your arm rubbing across my cheek

I want to know you from grass stains to fresh laundered sheets
I want to break with you, calcified in some distant fossil collective
I want your dust to be my dust
And for us to float across some empty room together
In an afternoon just like today

9.
Untethered
Unbound
Unable to port, to clasp, to dock
Lacking cohesivity
Teflonned
Untouchable
Sheathed
Repelling
Bordered by an unapproachable aura
A force field
A barricade
A battering ram
A barge
Drifting all away
An orbit
Some gravity
A universe between us
Thoughts telegraphed through dark matter

10.

When I dream it's that I'm fire
Suddenly waking up in ash
Purifying all who touch me
And blacking out the past
When I sleep it isn't pleasant
There's a crackle in my soul
This bed is an inferno
This present is just coal
The blast furnace is a shower
Cool to touch upon my face
My alarm clock is the sun
And when I'm done
I'll have won the human race

11.

Talking to you makes me feel raw
Like you were dead and now you're back
And I want to jump on you and ask you 18 million things
But I'm absolutely certain that'd make you go back to bed
You're someone who's held my heart in their hand
Like god gave you a key
And he didn't make too many of those
I feel like a fucking kid again
Nervous and alone
Excited to get five words from you
I hate it and I love it
And I sift through this all for seven minutes of you shining

12.

A Drawing In

Anyone can walk down my street
A conversation on the steps is nice
If I let you in the foyer, it's just to warm
So I could look at you
I've let ghosts in
Maniacs, thieves
What does that say about my home?
That for a while, the devil and I can be comfortable here?

Crocodile Cliko Cliko

It's probly not the place for you
Mostly it's just for me
Everyone else is just passing through

13.

The world needs poets
We're the ones standing out in the open with naked souls
Offering a reference point for the world to agree upon
That yes, there is a wonder to being human
That yes, there is some wonder even in the worst of us

14.

Do you know in movies
Where the main character
Has this room in their head
That's the projection of safety
And that's where their
Consciousness lives?
Mine is a razor
That's what I'm always coming back to
I don't feel depressed or suicidal
I don't even feel unstable
There's just a razor there
And when my mind drifts
And the scale of everything I am
Floats back to its natural position
A razor runs down the center of it all
I exhale calmly
I'm at peace

15.

Love is something beyond space and time
You can be in love with someone you've never met, just ask a nun
You can know someone your entire life
And never love or be in love with them
You can meet someone tomorrow
That person may be the love of your life
And you may only ever know them for a month
In the dimension of love that all makes sense

16.
Life weathers roads
Experience storms scars and grows flowers
We twist grow cover hills and soak mountains
Dead families fertilize the pastures of our soul
We climb trees there and look deep into the future
Hate is a rock in your shoe, a bee in your eye
Rest is where we plan our journeys
Love is a full belly and a warm coat
We keep moving

17.
Pass by every home
Hop fences over the cul-de-sac
Whistle through empty fields
Dodge trees
Follow the highway
Catch rides from strangers
Float across an ocean
Disembark
Hop on a train
Begin walking
Come to a desert
And take off

18.
I'd hate to ever be the center of any universe
I don't want moons or satellites
I prefer astronauts
Amazed at how high they can leap from my lack of gravity
If I shine or flicker or burn out
Don't worry about it
Don't colonize me
Don't cry when an asteroid hits
Just let me float
And if I don't explode
Maybe we'll bump into each other again
Sometime before everything ends

19.
I want to ink away into the night
And roll like clouds through porch lit towns
I want morning to find me teetering
On the lip of some strange canyon mouth
Eyes crusted, lids dusty
One hundred twenty paces past the tracks
Resting against a rock
So I can keep moving

20.
Just think. If your life is a mountain, every you in every moment, is
built up piled on top of each other, pulling in the entirety of your
surroundings to give you the gift of this you now to stand on.
That's called being present.

21.
Our lives are adrift in the elements
Who knows how we'll react to each other on any given day
Life is an alchemist in a tower, a parade of days, moments, molecules
Who knows where or when gold is going to turn up
And you can't fault explosions any more than you can the sea
For waving while water passes land

22.
Turn your head
Close your eyes
Turn the lights off
Don't look at me
Drift away
I'm disappearing
I pray your spotlight eyes fizzle
I'm in the dusk
Ready to fade

23.
I didn't write this
I put my pen to the paper
And let it bleed out
All you're reading is black
Pronounced in a void
On occasion, this tattoo may pixelate
Start to fade
If you put your hand to the paper
You're part of the death
It's a twilight zone
If you're eyes are skipping across letters
You've reached the border land
Take a deep breath
If the poem swallows you
It's okay
If you drown
It's okay
If you fall asleep
Sleep well
If you never wake up from the pillow book
Drift as you do
I'll keep reading

24.
People aren't roads to me anymore
They're doorways
Opening up to homes
Here you are in my doorway
We're not going anywhere
Maybe it's because I'm older, settled, broken in
Less interested in the transitory
I've crafted this home, hollowed out of a grove and lit a fire
What do you have in there? Let me see
I have calm   with space to run
A mania painted across the walls
A room to dance, a library
There's room to grow, a window
A place to die if I need to

Crocodile Cliko Cliko

I have a couch for weary travelers
People stop in off the road
They come and they go
I hope they leave rested, happier, well fed
At peace

25.

Sleep is a dark sea mirror
Looking to my eyes
And every wave crashing
Is a lash
Sliding down the glass
A wet hand on the sand
Is traveling through stars
And the ocean takes me
Deep into

26.

Acetylene Affairs
Every night there's this little piece of my stomach
That sinks in when you don't show up
Between us we've built cities and forests and mountain ranges
Your absence creates caverns
I get used to that sinking feeling
I don't think it's the end of the world
Every time the roof caves in
I know you'll fix it except for that one final time
You just don't come home
I guess that's when I'll crawl out from the crumble

27.

There's a corner in the chaos
Where I can sip my drink and watch you
Moving through the center of it all
The muscles in my hand involuntarily twitch
And think to reach for you
I haven't really cared for the songs that they've been playing
But the way you sway and twirl to horrible music
Makes the dj's crimes almost forgivable

You smile and pirouette
While I dream of walking out of here with you into the time storm
Of holding my coat over you through the years
Of kisses in the rain
And way better music
I could see you dancing somewhere less chaotic
Somewhere quiet
A living room A forest A parking lot
A corner in the chaos where songs are hummed and whispered
Somewhere dark we could share a drink

28.
I fucked a lonely girl
And caught a darkness in my soul
I think about sleeping now
In ways I hadn't thought before
Her sweat smelled like memories
Rusty and forgotten
Her wet soaked down to the bedrock
Left stains
Now I stay away from bathtubs and trains
At best I hope I took away her pain
But worst, I only lose it when someone
Comes to let it down the drain
And that sucks
But those are the breaks

29.
Every mind is a room
The door to which can only be opened
Onto another room
Some people spend their lives locked
Inside four walls
Some people run through mansions
And castles
They have libraries in other countries
Some rooms have windows
Some have showers
Some rooms are rest

Crocodile Cliko Cliko

My room has a spiral staircase behind the wall
A secret passage
My room is a portal
You should be careful about entering

30.
The sea in my chest never rises past the beach
It only waves as you walk on by
While other seas spill out over islands
And sweep away homes
My sea is self-contained
It sends post cards
A calm face in the sun
My sea would prefer you refrain from drowning please
It belongs only to me
It runs cold, miles deep
My sea has known earthquakes
And volcanos, asteroids
And nothing has consumed it
My sea breathes
It welcomes life
But is a life of its own
It has no interest in erosion
Or what your plans are for it
My sea is not an abyss
But it looks back into you just the same
My sea is a looking glass, a medium
An essence with borders defined by a current
My sea will always be

31.
Whatever your escape is
It's just a pillow in your cell at the edge of the universe
Your dream is just a distraction in the cycle
Whatever magic door you unlock
Only changes the dimensions of this house arrest
The highest highs are here
And I know you're thinking you can sneak out
To float in some oasis come 3am

But it's just another room
Even the mountains and oceans are walls
You've been sequestered like a toy dog
Alive for someone else's plans
So enjoy your joy
Drag your pillow to the corner
And taste how good sleep feels
Fall in love if you want
There's no slipping through the bars of this cage
You won't be happier out there drifting through a solace

32.
When the sun is off visiting its other family
I stop spinning and I ponder the timeline
An adolescence in chaos, the adoration of lonely souls
Ghosts in their bedrooms, moments stuck to the walls
A pink strawberry cake cooking in the oven, a junkie's smile
The growth that only comes from pain
Everything I ever wanted strewn out across the kitchen floor
There were drinks and lovers, guns to my head
There were perfect moments
Before I ever knew perfect moments existed
There were waves and particles
I know the sun is coming back again
I follow the horizon and look for cracks in the ether
I look for wormholes to reach through
My heart tends to magic, it pulses
Only me & God are in the room
From nothing we built this, and in the instant I stop looking
The divided de-sections
My kitchen river runs clocks across linoleum
Sunlight comes rushing through
I take a deep breath before being launched into orbit and unfreeze
But remember, you can always pause when you need to
If only to try and fathom your forever for a minute or two

33.
It's not that anyone is this character you've cast them as
That's just the way you see them
Because that's the way that's there for them to interact with you
To someone else they're a completely different person
And I love that about people
That they're a particle or a wave
Depending on if you're looking

34.
A Completion

That deep dive
That spark into a fire
It evades me
That falling off a cliff
That feels like flying
I set fires but they don't burn down cities
I jump off planes and land safely
No one has ever loved me so entirely
That they ate my body down to my soul
And try as I might to eat those I love
I always leave the table full

35.
There's a joy here, like a playground
That can't be wiped away
I reach out for you like a jungle gym
To run through like our childhood
Mine was a forest between two lakes
Bordered by horseradish & pussy willows
Easily lost in, haunted and full of secret caves
Yours spills out in diners
When the guards change shifts
Across your lips
I gather what I can
A candied treasure

36.

I have this internalized overwhelming demand to be loved
Burning like an unspoken rage every time we talk
Love me like I love you
My love leaks out, it can't be contained
Maybe you think that's what love is
My trickles, just precum
But my love is hell
It's a river of fire beneath an ocean of fire
A firefall dropping down a trench
Melting the face off a hydrogen bomb
Praying to a liquid god
For the sun to be submerged in some reciprocity
I want us to burn when I swallow you
I want a love collapsed like the death of a black hole
Where everything between us is expunged
And fire is the only story left to read

37.

Tell me how you've grown over the years
Lay here on my chest at breath's length
Let me inhale the dreams you've mixed with memories
Smudges I'dve never forgotten
A pool hall painted in the blackest black
A bra strap never unsnapped
Unfold your story for me
Ferry me across a child I met walking into adulthood
Unto a hero on their quest
Read me to sleep
So the story's never finished

38.

I've been carving a secret behind this door for 30 years now
I've been gnawing at the marrow of dark matter
Worshiping our mother of the universe
In a sweaty amniotic bed
Finger scars where stars are born

Crocodile Cliko Cliko

I've been singing to god
And summoning an apocalypse from the ether
I've been breathing in the ears of witches
Fucking them towards forsaking the unholy
I've been crying with angels
And eating ice cream with children
I've been born at the blast site
And born again
Sucked a soul off of fingers
Coiled around some hyperventilation
I've plunged where you've fluttered
Like some epileptic demigod
Alone in the dark stuttering Morse code arc light
In this ritual music box I flirted with a little death
And bade an orgy towards our genocide
This is the first silhouette I've ever offered
I'm unseen

39.
There is no story to tell
Every morning you wake up
And every night you go into the dark
Rarely you'll appreciate exactly what you have
Mostly you'll appreciate things in their absence
Joy will come in great streams
You won't be able to contain it
It'll form the valleys and peaks of your life
The streams will become a drought
And you'll find your home in the dust
Strangers will approach you
Telling you there's a life beyond the desert
But this is your life
You slide out of one human body to begin
And you end drifting from your own
Savor it like moist cake
Gone when you swallow
Your body will turn against you
Your mind will turn against you

Your spirit will be trapped like a channel between signals
Electricity, but not lightning, just static
And when the switch is flipped
You won't even be a dead star in the sky
You'll just be gone

40.
As long as you run
As far as you make it
Pieces of you will end up
In the trail of carrion running parallel

As fast as you are
As strong as you've been
Scar tissue will take the place of muscle
And your strength will be just to know
That only one thing ever kills you

41.
If a mountain is alive and crumbles
Then all the broken rock parts of the mountain are alive
The life in them that makes them one's self
Is the life that was the mountain
So it is with men and animals as well
And that life is god
And god has not crumbled but bloomed
God pollinates god and more god blossoms
This is where both the reason and request for kindness stems from
For god's feelings are hurt when god
Again and again goes on hurting god
But we keep drawing lines between the rocks and the mountain

42.
Power is like a body of water
You can stand on the edge of it
You can swim in it
You can sail across it
You can choose your battles
Harness your resources

Crocodile Cliko Cliko

And build a dam
A channel, a desalination plant
You can eat from it
You can poison it
You can dive deep
And meet the million creatures
Who call it their home
You can stare in awe at it
You can memorialize the houses it took
And the soldiers it swallowed
But the bigger the body
The less likely it is to disperse
Power gathers
It forms in clouds
And runs in drops
Down windows and cups of tea
It starts in puddles
Gathers in ditches
And meets in a system of waterways
That always touch the ocean
Power is stored over centuries
On mountain tops
Despite babies being thirsty
Despite the nations who need it
Despite the fact that power is unequally dispersed
Some people live on islands
Surrounded by power
Their whole lives are a pool in a sailboat aquarium
While others live in deserts
Savoring what little power they have
Horribly unaware of the fact that their body is 70% water
Taking for granted that they're alive
A body of power
Self-contained
But so much more when they have a friend
When they make a group
When they stream into the streets
And become an ocean of people
Some people taste a little power

Unaware of how water grows
And others drown in it
Remembering that first drop on their lips
Like a wet dream
Some people just drift away

43.
Writing is an attempt at control
To pin something down
To understand it
To give form in a void

44.
We're on a spinning ball
In an enormous collection of spinning balls
Formed and warmed by gas & explosions
We're so determined to not float away

45.
Having been born and raised in chaos
As an adult I find myself longing for the home of my youth
Every night I wait for a knock on the door, unstable actors
A text and I'm ready to jump into the dark
Waves crashing, buildings falling, it's normal to me
But here I am, stuck in a boat on the Sargasso Sea
Waiting for a storm, ready to walk home

46.
Time is coming like ocean breaths
Breaking over this importance
Washing it all away
And dissolving the current
Into dissipated life
Crumbling towards the trench
Never to be sifted through

47.
When you say you can't believe in the spiritual because of science,
all I hear is that you lack imagination and have only the vaguest
notion of what science is, a hunger to understand set about on rails
and launched towards the unknown. You're feeble. I'll pray for you.

48.
Lately, I've just been sitting out here on the bottom step
Staring down the path
Clutching my book and watching the tornadoes coming
Everything is a twirly turvy
We can't really build the way we'd like
Even the pages flip and I can't keep my story straight
I don't feel like the main character here
There's no love interest
There hasn't been for a long time
The author tried introducing several female leads but nobody stuck
I don't know that these stairs will take me anywhere
I can't say for certain there's a home here
I don't wish anyone to walk along this path
I don't know that I've met anyone I can trust
Anywhere close to as much as I trust myself

Cars fly through houses, fathers die, sisters get divorced
I'd love to get out of the way
I'd love to lead us all to safety
I wish I could move faster but I'm locked in, a spirit bound to the path
It's who I am. I have to take each step
I can't go anywhere but where the road leads
My moments are dictated by the author's engine
Combusting forward our speed of play
I often wonder who's telling this story and marvel at how it unfolds
One day I'll turn my last page
Who knows where we'll be
But my story will be finished if not complete
My path will become abandoned
Overgrown with wild leaves, obscured
And you'll have closed the book on me

Part 3:

1.

I like hearing people's stories of what they did as teenagers. Some people learned to play guitar or studied really hard or hung out with their friends and partied. I walked around LA, often in the dark. I memorized bus lines and spent my free time walking down side streets in Elysian Park, Temple City, El Sereno, Venice. I walked every corner of Long Beach. I combed Lynwood. I memorized South Gate over and over, its rooftops, it's alleys.

I crisscrossed Downey, hopping fences, grabbing oranges, hiding under cars. I walked Bell, Bell Gardens, Cudahy. I'd catch a bus to who the fuck knows where, Whittier and wander. That's what I did with my teenage years. I found it fascinating that all these places existed. That all of them were somewhere I could go. That bus lines and streets were like veins and if I took the time I could learn the body.

I covered, Cerritos, Lakewood, Paramount, West Hollywood, Santa Monica, Downtown LA, Anaheim, La Palma. So many cities. LA is huge and time never stops. I didn't steal. I don't know anyone most of these places. Sometimes I prayed or read, occasionally I wrote graffiti but honestly mostly I just walked every inch of Los Angeles I could, like the only direction I ever had in life was to wander.

I'd walk through Watts like I had a reason to be there other than this is where the train dropped me off. Do you know how many feet of sidewalk there are between any two people in LA? 9,300 miles of it. There's 9,300 miles of sidewalk here. I wonder how many I've hit. How many miles I've done.

I remember my mom picking me up from Torrance in the middle of the night. It was raining so hard and I didn't know how to get back home. Buses stopped running. I called from a pay phone and while I was waiting this guy pulled up and told me Jesus didn't love me, because I was ugly, then he spit at me. Sometimes things like this would happen.

Sometimes I'd leave the house in a huff with no shoes and walk through Bellflower trying to remember where this girl I knew lived and ended up at my cousin's house, where I crashed shoeless and walked home shoeless. If a bus came, I'd hop on the bus but who knew if the bus would ever come. You couldn't wait too long. It was safer to make the long trek from Carson, through North Long Beach all the way to Lakewood Mall than it was to sit there and wait for a bus that never came.

I walked for fucking ever. It wasn't necessary. Now my legs are tired but I can't get new ones. So I just ache and walk less. When I was a kid out there, roaming, no one ever took me home. Once in a great while luck would give me a ride and that was better than a home. If I wanted a home, I'd of stayed in my own.

My mom says it's her fault for putting me on a plane by myself as a four year old across country. But I remember roaming before that. The first thing I recall is jumping out of my bedroom window when I was three years old, and landing on a duck egg. I wore a cowboy hat and drove a tricycle. I rode my tricycle onto the freeway. Later I crossed the country at 18 on my own. I made it from Chicago to LA in 20 hours, peeing in a bottle of Mountain Dew as I drove.

In college, I worked for a traveling veterinary clinic. LA still impressed me. I never made it to the valley till then, or Malibu, Shadow Hills, La Cañada, more and more places. Eventually LA showed me the door, I was tired of it here. I moved to Australia and started learning Sydney, the back streets of Paddington, Darlinghurst, Surrey Hills was a labyrinth that made no sense to me. But eventually I learned it. I mastered the grid and moved on, traveled the world. So life prepared me for the fact that there are no answers anywhere.

My apprenticeship was forged in a pile of bus schedules for cheap in MacArthur Park. My garden is transitory lonely moments, seeds growing seeds till I die one day a tree who fell asleep. A pillowbook. Sometimes I wonder who will stop to read me.

2.

I recently started reading this book on genetics a friend recommended. It's pretty interesting. First of all, we all come from Africa. Secondly, before modern humans were the Neanderthals, and even though modern humans sometimes bred with Neanderthals, the old model died out. Sometimes I have conversations with Neanderthals and I wonder how they snuck through with these outdated concepts. Because some of the shit people are talking in light of the recent movement to end police brutality and have some fucking equality especially to be inclusive of a people who've been brutalized on this land since they were enslaved and brought here against their will makes me hope I see the day people that think in the old hateful brainwashed way are completely extinct and the sea change we find ourselves in where power is being revoked and redistributed brings us to a whole 'nother land. The civil war here right now is one of mind and spirit. Don't side with hate. Side with love.

3.

The first time I met a stranger from the internet was at a punk show at The Troubadour. She was a big Korean girl who went to UCLA. Not big like fat, big as in she looked like she could body slam you if need be. She was the first of thousands. Before a year had passed I married one of those strangers. Every girl I ever loved was a stranger at some point. My first experience couchsurfing, I had lunch in Tijuana with this girl named Adriana. This was back when the cartels were wild. Crossing the border both ways took no time at all. We were lucky. No one was shooting that day but the city was a ghost town. It was raining. We had a really beautiful day. I started counting at one so I can tell you, 482 strangers have slept on my couch and strangers the world over have let me in their homes, fed me, cared for me like family. I know the world can be a horribly scary place but I don't see it that way. I see everyone just trying to be happy.

I do my best to give them what they want and this happiness between us all has been my key, unlocking the world to me. I started this as a note and really didn't intend to babble on like this but I just wanted to thank every single stranger I've ever met. You've become my best friend, my happiness, my lovers, my brothers, my treasure, the spirit of all goodness haunting me. May you find the treasure in everyone yourself and may you be eternally rich. Thank you.

4.

There is no other person who will fulfill you. You won't ever be perfect. Life is always going to be full of problems. You are a ghost and you will haunt this world for eternity. If you can accept this, if you can be ok with being incomplete, if you can use the broken you, you will find that life is beautiful. It can be fun and an amazing adventure. If you can accept this you'll see that your broken incompleteness is the whole state of an amazing entity, capable of incalculable goodness. Don't worry about finding a person. That feeling is a biological drive to recreate that's programmed into your core software. Don't worry about being your best best you. That bar will always be out of your reach. Just live this life. That's a lot. It's a whole lifetime's worth.

5.

Why is your response to "black lives matter" when a young black man who plays the violin for cats is killed while walking home from getting an iced tea, that all lives matter? Why is your response to "black lives matter" when a black nurse is gunned down in her bed by police at the wrong house, blue lives matter? Why when 1,000 people are killed yearly by police do you fight the cries for change? Why do you blame those outraged in the streets for being abused? Why are you okay with little kids being separated from their parents & put in cages? Why does a celebrity with 25 sexual assault allegations become president? Why do you watch a man die over the course of nine minutes and blame him for dying? Why are the cries for affordable health care and education objects of scorn for you? Why do you wave a loser's flag? Why do you equate a 2,000 year old religion of kindness taught by a homeless immigrant with being the foundation of a country built on slavery and greed? Why are you offended by a three letter word?

6.

Here I am. Back to 1. Looking at the hole and thinking of better ways to climb it. Passing clouds remind me of those who've been down here in the dark with me, such good friends. For years, they've been living somewhere in my stomach and I want to pull them through. If memories are energy and energy is matter then these people are alive in the moments between souls, stuck in the crannies of a braincell, knocking on the windows of your memory, something your cat watches out the corner of its eye. All ghosts are welcome to climb this hole with me. I've found the haunting helps lubricate some synchronicity. See, I've been stretching and growing and feeding my aura. I flipped a switch like the kitchen light and became a beacon, attracting all the weird ones society says are unlatchable. I laid down and left a light on for them. I'm riding the wings of moths fresh out of dreams and licking their dust off my fingers. I'm tallying matchstick towers towards coincidence, trying to burn brighter, working at becoming a better daylight, trying to become today tomorrow.

7.

They call it coming down. I call it, I used to make strangers scream and smile. I used to make people happy. I used to be a spectacle when the music played. I used to drag a stage through every conversation and before the spot could fade I'd shoot the lights out. I used to have corners of the universe with god on my side, miles of sand & waves and just me. I used to have the privilege of surfing across people's palms, of really getting to know someone. I used to care when I met you, each and every one of you. You meant something to me. I used to dive off cliffs, sail seas, climb mountains, jump out of airplanes and never ask anyone for anything. I used to take a hit and not be afraid to take another one. I used to live off of kindness. I used to be as pure and innocent as a normal human being can be. Ain't that sad?

Now I'm needy. I need to eat. I need this roof. I need this job. I need to keep shit going. I need this to work. I need you to see me, to really really see me and I need you to turn away. I need a break. I need something to stick. I need like six months of not sitting at a desk, looking at a screen. I need to come to some sort of equilibrium. I need to go to bed at 10pm, do yoga and lose a minimum of 50 pounds. I need to study my languages because if I don't maintain consistency in this one teeny tiny aspect of my life then I might shuffle off. I need to stay in and not dance because I broke my foot twice and my nose once then my knee and now I'm fucking fragile. I need to not fall apart man. I need to hold this shit together. I need to give up on ever finding anyone who gets me that I get too because sifting through them all is draining and I need to protect myself. I need you to like this, to share this. I need you. Ain't that sad?

8.

The spirits call. They text. They make big shows of little things. So maybe one day I'll say what? What do you want? What is this way hidden from my earthly eyes. But I sigh. I see the way. I know the way. I breathe the way. I walk it like my every step was made to navigate, to glide, to climb. The veins from my heart run out my feed and I bleed the way. My little drummer boy sits in the lap of god. We dance like flames on the sun. We sail adrift on the current of solar radiation, riding thoughts dripping from the eyes of the architect who built this. My fingers skim along the face of god, surfing an ocean of tear waves. Now tell me, offer me a treasure map and a flashlight. Whisper me a secret. Give me a dream. Try and pry me away from what pulls on me like opposite ends of the earth and ask yourself if magnetism is word enough or must something else be invented to let you know how unattracted I am to anything you're offering.

9.

Dyu know that book, Slaughterhouse Five, where he's kind of adrift in time? I feel like that, like I've crammed 50 lives into this one and now I'm just adrift on the ocean of them. It's not hard to retell a story. I float through my own life every day. One moment, I'm a young man in love, the next I'm in jail, the next someone's dying. I'm just sticking my fingers in the water and riding the wave in this life-boat. I remember everything.

10.

Not sex, not love, not respect, not money or power or fame but joy is what I want. It's difficult to design your way into. It can't be earned. It tastes best when stumbled upon, like lost treasure in the street. It's inconstant. It can't be sustained outside a bubble. Perfect moments could come from anywhere. They don't last for long in and of themselves but they're what makes everything worth going through.

I've found a sincere openness and a willingness to experience whatsoever the moment has in hand can be the best kindling. Often a fire is ignited in madness, a rejection of the norm, a game, some imagination. You can lie for fun. Joy closes doors. It puts up barriers. New ways must be found inside it all the time. Joy is the heart of life but life has a body, a brain, it shits, it rests and all of life is fighting for dominance. You can't be a heart all the time. You must sleep and shit and even in these, joy is possible but never automatic.

The older I get, the more concerned I am with paying my rent. Having left home several times, I've found that coming back is the hardest resurrection. I'm afraid of being homeless, of being lonely, of living in pain. I've cultivated a middle class middle age wherein my greatest risk is accumulated debt ...and I still fight for joy. I'm constructing where I said no constructs will take you there and I still look for joy. I pray and pray and pray for joy but I dance less. I've closed my doors. There's no strangers to embrace. Mystery is hiding. I stopped turning over rocks. I have a routine now. I don't wander so much anymore but I still stumble hoping to trip over what makes me happy. I still carry a lighter. I'm ready to burn the city down if joy is in the ashes. I'm ready to be a chimney sweep if joy burned long ago. I still keep my sincerity open but the hallway to my heart is long. I've fallen over clasped hands and broken teeth that were not joy. I've seared my flesh and it didn't make me happy. I've jumped off bridges waiting to be embraced but stood up broken, and trudged away.

I fucked in the snow. I spit blood into my friends mouthes from across the room. I've screamed in a god's ear and told a baby he will always be a liar hoping that some joy might come of it. I've been ready but there are somethings I won't try again even though maybe joy is waiting in them. Mostly I lay here and remember treasures I've had, perfect moments joy has given me. I collect them to my chest, joy haunts me. I wouldn't trade joy for anything. In everything I see all around me, the only question I ever have is, "how might joy come of this?"

11.

Mojave roads of the spirit, taking whip turns at ninety miles an hour while you smile at God, worshiping the grey orange dusk of his paintbrush just isn't the same as making a stranger a friend, a friend a lover, and biting off some tiny part of them to dissolve and mix into the life stew of your acid bath soul.

Would you take an adventure with me? I've never had a fist fight. I've never smoked hashish or laughed at bodily fluids in an orgy. I've fallen in love and don't know how many times I can do it again. I've rained down joy. I've set dreams on fire. I've walked away from perfect moments just to honor them. I've given myself. I've taken less than I need. I've savored the taste of my own vomit and drove a diesel truck through a warehouse full of hourglass.

Order & Chaos are best friends and I love to haunt them. I wear their scars like bracelets and headbands. Their trauma hangs from silver hairs I stopped plucking like a century's worth of sacrifice dangling over the crossroads. If boring needs a devil I'll meet you there. I'll be your adversary. I'm selling all of this for just a tiny piece of your soul.

The tears that come when my teeth take are mine too. Remember this fragment when you become me. Remember that no one ever wanted you the way that I do.

12.

Imagine I were able to recreate meeting a shining soul in the street, the giant backpack strapped to her as she stopped me in Chinatown to ask for directions, the durian being chopped at a stall nearby, tiny yellow bananas. Imagine me persuading her towards an adventure, bread crumbs back to my hostel, her smile that never stops, beers clinking, us at 4am desperately thirsting for sleep, thrust into the predawn Kuala Lumpur bustle like toes sticking out of cold sheets, our taxi to the airport, me changing my ticket at the last minute to follow her wherever she's going. Screw Borneo. Where are you going again? So I buy the ticket. I soak her in and stare and hang on the stories of her old Chinese mother forcing the foulest black potion down her throat, of a weekend in Tel Aviv, floating on the Dead Sea, of shady deals done in Dubai and having to flee. It's crazy to ponder a trepidation under the pinkest calm.

We climbed ruins. I clung to her voice. I was all in. Perhaps the most effectively placed term one could use here would be enchanted. If humans aren't magic, I don't know what is. We rode bicycles through the jungle at dusk, racing monkeys for Coca-Cola and bribing children with dollar bills to be our friends.

Phnom Penh hit us in a flood. Nothing but rain and she & I locked in a room talking about our sisters, our tragedies and what food we missed the most. I had to walk out, midcalf deep in the puddles of French IndoChine just to keep from eating her. There's no cinnamon roll I remember never having stuck between my teeth like the girl I left safely in a room behind the waterfall Cambodia because she was too valuable and I'm no good at playing it safe.

If I told you all that, you still wouldn't know half the story but you could imagine.

13.

Have you ever fallen in love with the wrong person? You're human, of course you have. I fell in love once, like a ringlet wrapped around their finger. And even though I've uncurled, their stripes stain my mirror. This streak persists. It's not so easily wiped away. Since the day dark tapped the glass on my incubator and offered a hand, we've been strolling this human body of water, deep and beautiful, immense and unexplained. You skim the surface, you learn the wet, you dive right in and every time you come up for air you remember what it's like to be submerged. Every bath is blissfully unaware of what's within reach. There's a current that will take you to the cave but some knowledge is never ascertained. From before even my parents were born, dark had been grooming some shape of me, like a father in the shadows with waves in his chalice, holding my hand at the pool. So romantic. When I swam to shore, bruised, scarred, ears ringing with a siren song, I dragged myself from the edge of the earth and turned to see my friends drowning and I questioned this love that's all consuming because I'm nobody's sacrifice.

14.

Racism is an exclusivity
Any exclusivity is a disregard
Any disregard for life harms life
By setting in motion destruction simply because it fails to protect
Isolation creates intangible boundaries
That forms an identity based on an experience
Which is intrinsically exclusionary
To close off is to kill
To be open, to include, is to protect
Thus any border between peoples serves only
To exclude life from protection

15.

The most normal line of reasoning is that this great big blue green ball of ice and rock is just a warm cage/habitat/aquarium. It's just a place. For the most part, you walk when it's day, you sleep when it's night and the only real difference between the two is your perception. But I have a hypothesis that when my eyelids drop there's a door opening and whole other worlds are walked through, floated in, dreamed upon, the feather world. Its laws are physics fluid, bound only to the mind. It bends like mercury between synapses. Its foundation is set on cushions. Its clouds atmosphere about, inhaled in cycles throughout the day. My breaths rise like incense offered up to the god who dreamed me. My dreams sleep less and less and less. They scorch and teethe. The sore between worlds is opened and never healing. It oozes pillow waves crashed on sandy day shine eye cusps. We're just sleepwalking on the beach, trying to make sense of it all.

16.

Today is my little sister's birthday. I love her so much. She's my oldest friend. Having a sibling teaches you some of life's most important lessons. That love is ongoing not ascertained. That you may struggle and disagree with the person you love, that someone else can come from the exact set of dna and places as you, have the same experiences and be a complete individual, different from yourself. My sister is definitely an individual. I have admired and wondered at her my entire life. She's vividly and forcefully alive. I've always been amazed at that. I admire how her person contrasts that with an innate fragility. I admire how she's always growing and always giving and always concerned with both of those things. I've learned from her about motherhood and appreciating our own mother. I learn from her all the time. There's no other person I would want in her place. I feel so lucky to have been through this entirety with her. I can't wait to see where she's going and who she continues to grow into being. Happy birthday Pooh.

17.

People who preach that we need to seize the day, and live life in every moment to its fullest are just addicted to their body's own reactions to external stimuli. The only difference between them and a drug addict is that their body makes the drugs instead of factory workers in India. You are literally as alive as you'll ever be whether you're skydiving or working at a desk. You're in every moment you're in. It's just some moments are crackers and some are candy. Some lives are mulch and some are acid. Some living beings are humans and some are ants. Some people like to think they're better than others while some just live their lives.

18.

Some people walk the periphery of your labyrinth
Knowing the spirit of your forest wants to drag them deeper
Some people end up broken
Pounding on the door of an enchanted castle
Sobbing about a dream
Some people end up living in a sunny day
Blissed out at your pool but have to leave
You never know where you'll end up
When you get lost in a person

19.

When I was a little kid. We lived at a large apartment complex
in Oklahoma between two lakes. I used to go out and play at the lake
every day, catch crawdads, run through the pussy willows and walk
through the forest. There was supposed to be an old man who lived in
the forest and the kids say he'd chase you with a spear. I did see him
once but he never chased me. I think he was just a regular ass old
man. One day though I was down at the lake catching crawdads and
these older kids started to play with me. I was 7 and they were like 11.
I didn't know them but apparently they lived right there by the lake so
they took me inside to show me some toys. This is how I ended up
hogtied and gagged, crying in a locked room while they looked me
over with a knife. They decided to let me go and the difference
between being tortured and being free lived in some child's whim.
I've never been afraid of old men as much as I have of children. I've
seen children do all sorts of fucked up shit. It's weird that adults
forget that. Maybe I just grew up swimming in a bad pool.

20.

When I slept with Jenni that weekend and she had 25 orgasms
There was this like 15 minutes that were perfect. The sky was grey.
We stared out the window looking at the trees and the mountains and
the freeway in the twilight while the Innocence Mission played and it

was calm and lovely and she laid on my chest and the world was peaceful and perfect for several breaths. No romance.
Just two humans.

21.

Whether you're alone, 400 miles from the nearest human or wrapped up inside someone, the earth spins in a dark sea of stars and you get a lifetime, whether it be 4, 27 or 100 years. More than likely you'll be stuck on something small, something human, because human is all you can be. Like dogs sniff shit, we spend our lives bound to the course plotted for us. Some brave souls want us to be the best humans we can be and way too many are the worst …but there's skin and space and time, those are the parameters. Everything you bounce off of: love & joy, the spirit realm, a real connectivity, a sense of peace and fulfillment; these are the targets of being human.
A hierarchy of being is just the levels of the game and one day you will die. So play the game however you see fit. Good luck.

22.

Don't ever think that god doesn't love you
God is love
We as limited beings can't understand
Something without limits
We try to model God after our own
Idealized pattern of behavior and
Fit God into the thoughts we can manage
And then we get mad when God doesn't fit
Because we're small
And hate to accept that our lives
Aren't the most important thing ever
Life on this planet is small
Which isn't to say that it's not beautiful or amazing
I myself am devoted to it
But life on this planet is just a drop
And we're just an atom in a drop
Screaming that we're so much more

Crocodile Cliko Cliko

Humanity is a tantrum
An ant begging God to love it like an ant
When God loves Infinitely beyond our understanding

23.

The body is a temple
Bow down at the altar
In this house of spirits
Where I've lived my entire life
And tour my haunted home

Uncle Cameron was a tennis star
You couldn't say anything bad about him
When the ice cream truck stopped
He made sure all the little kids were taken care of
I dunno if it was the eighties sex and drugs that got him
Or if he was raped while working in the middle east
Maybe depression just runs in my family
But he put a gun in his mouth and pulled the trigger
When I was ten years old
That was when death stopped me in the street to introduce itself

His brother Mark was a heroin addict
A liar, a robber, a drunk, a victim, abused, tortured
He was all the bad and all the good a person could ever be
He was hilarious & handsome, charismatic, engaging
A rockstar on his own merit, and a horrible asshole too
But I loved him
He overdosed at his ex-wife's house
After learning that he had aids
He cleaned his room, packed his bag, put on a suit
And grabbed the golden ticket
When his son came home and saw him sitting in a recliner
One of his friends said
Damn Kenny, it looks like your dad is dead
He was barely mourned but I miss him
I see him in the mirror everyday

Justin was a gang member
But saying that is like saying
Jesus had a beard and not really mentioning anything else
Justin was the center of a solar system
His block and all of South Gate circled him
Justin was bigger than giants
He was a genius. People worshipped him
But his dad was crazy
And the ghetto is most often the wrong place at the wrong time
After cutting records, pacing prison cells
And some sense of freedom
Justin went back to robbery. He killed a guy and had to flee
He became a truck driver. Then started robbing truck stops
He didn't want to go back to prison
So when the cops caught up with him
He pulled a gun and they filled him full of lead
We were never allowed to see the body
It was full of bullet holes

His brother Aaron was a baby
I adored that child
He was fire wrapped around a teddy bear
Nobody cared like him
I wish he would've made it
But he came home from work one day
and closed the bedroom door
His mother came to knock and tell him she made cookies
A minute later his brains were on the wall
Nobody knows why
He would've been thirty today

Their sister Priscilla came out for his funeral
She was smart & funny & cool and a good fucking soul
A few months later her husband murdered her
because she was leaving him after she found out he cheats
She walked away and he shot her in the back
Then shot himself in the stomach and waited to die
He got on Facebook and said what he did
Some friends came to kick the door open

Crocodile Cliko Cliko

He blew his brains out before they got in
The whole thing was on the news
I remember her funeral too much
It's so weird what a vivacious person looks like
When their life has left them

My grandmothers both just gave up at some point
June got a broken heart at fifty and that was it
She resigned to sit in her lazy boy wearing a mumu
Clutching the remote control
She just ate her life away
Mercy lost her husband, hit a slow decline
And just snowballed till the weight crushed her

Now I cling to those I love
I don't know if I can lose anymore
I've never had a very big house
I guess at some point
I'm gunna have to start doubling up rooms on ghosts
Because I can't afford to move out

24.

You can only go in one direction
And at the end you fall apart